VISION BOARD
CLIP ART BOOK
FOR BLACK TEEN GIRLS

🎁 YOUR FREE GIFTS

As a token of appreciation for your purchase, I'm excited to offer you four valuable bonuses:

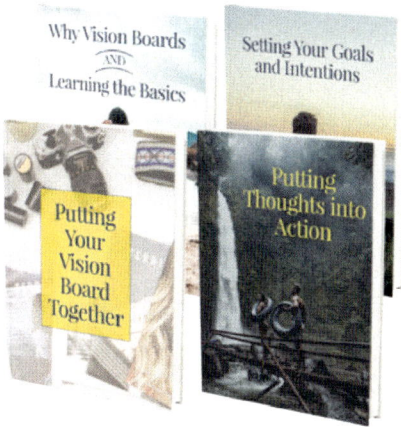

#1: "Creating Your Dream Life with Your Own Vision Board" (Course)

Unlock the potential within you and start manifesting your aspirations with my exclusive vision board course. Set clear intentions and turn your dreams into reality.

#2: "86 Quick & Easy Strategies for Saving Money" (eBook)

Discover 86 practical and easy-to-implement strategies to save money, budget wisely, and achieve your financial goals. This eBook is an indispensable guide for securing your financial future.

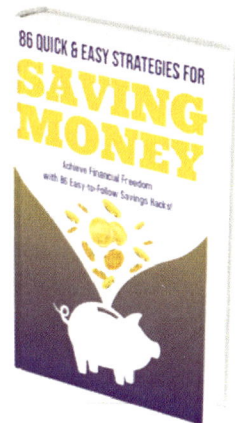

#3: "Teach Your Kids to Create Their Future with a Vision Board" (eBook)

Ideal for parents and mentors, this eBook provides essential techniques for teaching younger siblings or family members the power of vision boarding. It is designed to guide adults and older teens in fostering goal-setting and visualization skills in children.

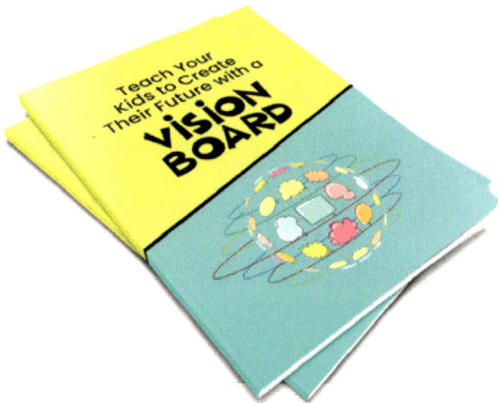

To access the first three gifts, sign up for my email newsletter for instant access at threegifts.kalishiawinston.com. Alongside these gifts, you will also receive tips, free book giveaways, discounts, and so much more.

#4 "Vision Board Clip Art Book for Black Teen Girls" (Printable PDF)

Inside the Vision Board Clip Art Book for Black Teen Girls, you'll find a treasure trove of inspiring clip art elements to fuel your dreams and creativity. But what if you need extra copies for a vision board party or want to retry cutting out an element? No worries!

Simply enter the link to access the PDF file, ready for printing (*no email sign-up required*): blackgirlvision.kalishiawinston.com

All of these bonuses are completely free and come with no strings attached. For the first three gifts, you only need to provide your email address. Enjoy your free gifts, and here's to nurturing dreams and achieving personal goals!

REFLECT AND ENVISION
Guiding Questions for Your Journey

As you embark on creating your vision board, it's important to think deeply about who you are, where you want to go, and what you want to achieve. These reflection questions are designed to inspire you and guide your vision board creation process. Take some time to journal your answers or simply ponder these questions to gain clarity and focus.

Who You Are and What You Value

1. What makes you feel the most empowered and why?
2. Describe a day in your life five years from now. What does it look like?
3. What are three things you love about yourself?
4. What hobbies or activities make you lose track of time?
5. Who do you look up to, and what qualities do they have that you admire?

Facing Fears and Embracing Growth

6. If fear was not a factor, what would you try today?
7. What are you most grateful for in your life right now?
8. What are your top three priorities in life at this moment?
9. How can you make a positive impact on your community?
10. What does success mean to you?

Setting Goals and Dreaming Big

11. What are three goals you have for this year?
12. What qualities do you want to be known for?
13. If you could change one thing about the world, what would it be?
14. What are you most passionate about? How can you do more of that?
15. What does your ideal friendship or relationship look like?

Leveraging Strengths and Overcoming Challenges

16. What are your biggest strengths, and how can you use them more?
17. What is something new you'd like to learn or try out?
18. How do you handle setbacks and challenges?
19. When do you feel the most confident?
20. What does a balanced life look like to you, and how can you achieve it?

Feel free to return to these questions as often as you like. They can serve as a powerful tool to remind you of your strengths, dreams, and the path you are paving for yourself. Each time you revisit them, you might find your answers change as you grow and evolve.

Enjoy the process of discovery, and let these questions guide you as you create a vision board that truly reflects your dreams and aspirations.

GIRL POWER

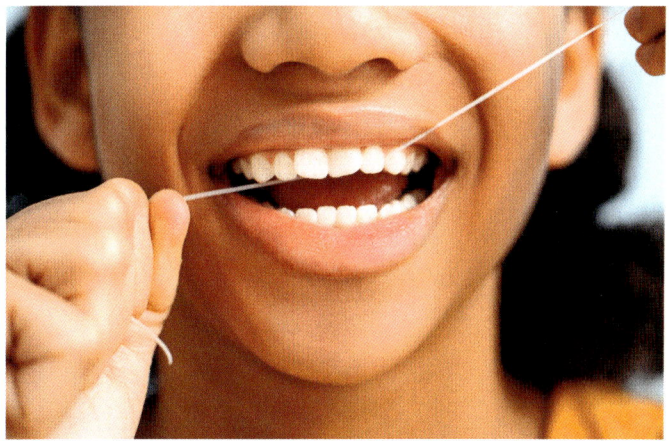

Embrace
SELF-CARE

LOVE your Body

BALANCE

INNER PEACE

MINDFULNESS

Friends Forever

Trust & Love

FAMILY FIRST

TOGETHER
ALWAYS

My Family

Educate & Elevate

STRIVE FOR EXCELLENCE

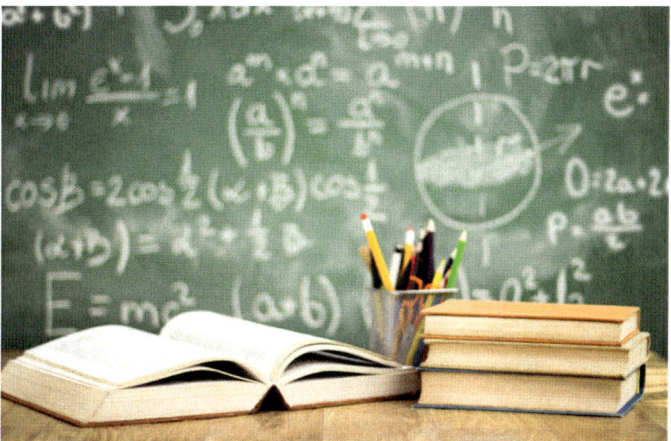

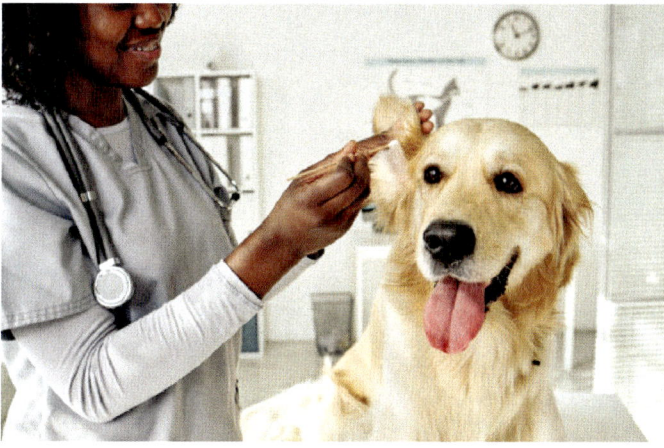

PURSUE PASSION

DREAM FEARLESSLY

EMPOWERED ENTREPRENEUR

#girlboss

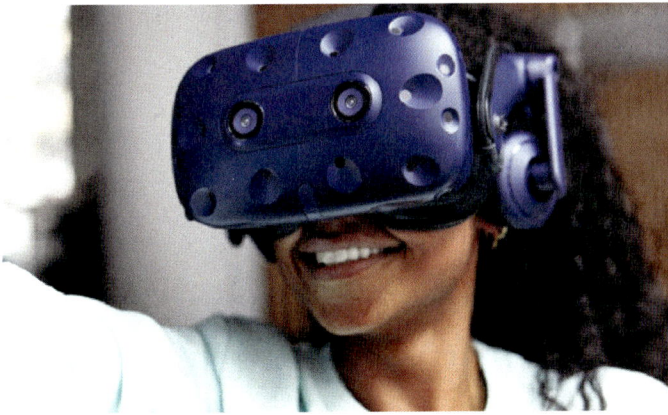

PROGRAMMING Technology

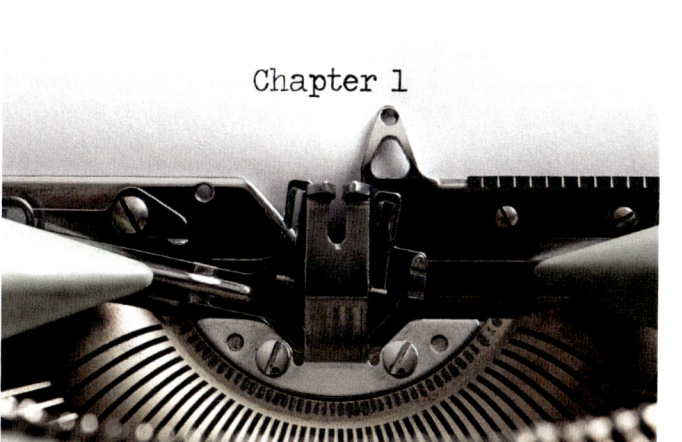

Chapter 1

Color Your World

CREATE & INSPIRE

DANCING

Keep moving forward.

DANCE

SEWING

FASHION

Stay True   Beauty

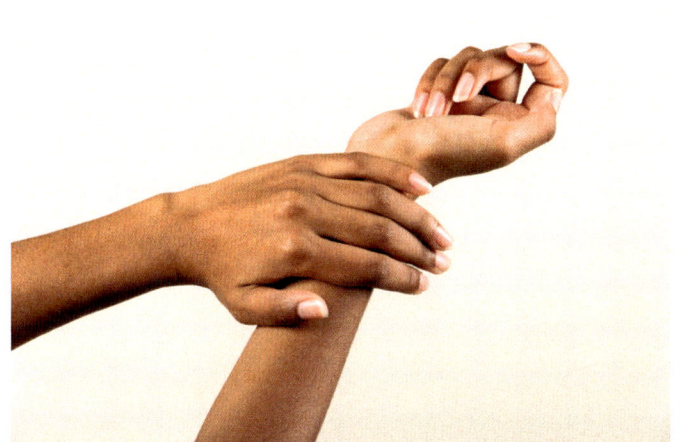

FITNESS FOR LIFE

STAY ACTIVE

BE THE EXAMPLE *Kindness Matters*

Explore & Learn | TRAVEL

DISCOVER AMERICA *Road Trip*

Craft Your Brand

GO VIRAL

I MAKE SMART MONEY CHOICES FOR MY FUTURE

BUDGET SMART

Grow Your Wealth

CELEBRATE

MAKE MEMORIES

I AM STRONG, CAPABLE,
AND UNSTOPPABLE
IN PURSUING MY DREAMS

MY VOICE IS POWERFUL
AND MY STORY MATTERS

I AM A QUEEN, DESERVING
OF RESPECT AND LOVE
FROM MYSELF AND OTHERS

EVERY DAY, I GROW
MORE CONFIDENT
AND COURAGEOUS

I AM A LEADER, SHAPING
MY FUTURE WITH EVERY
CHOICE I MAKE

I EMBRACE MY CULTURE,
CELEBRATING THE BEAUTY
AND STRENGTH IT ADDS
TO MY IDENTITY

MY POTENTIAL IS
LIMITLESS, AND I RISE
ABOVE ANY CHALLENGE

I AM SURROUNDED BY LOVE
AND SUPPORT, ALWAYS

I INVEST IN MYSELF BY
NURTURING MY BODY,
MIND, AND SPIRIT

I ATTRACT POSITIVE
OPPORTUNITIES THAT
HELP ME GROW AND THRIVE

MY UNIQUENESS IS MY
SUPERPOWER, AND I
CELEBRATE IT EVERY DAY

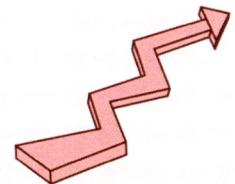

EVERY STEP I TAKE IS
A STEP TOWARDS MAKING
MY DREAMS A REALITY

I LEAD WITH GRACE AND COURAGE, TRANSFORMING CHALLENGES INTO OPPORTUNITIES

Voice Your Opinions	Support Others	Act with Integrity
Spread Kindness	I Am Peaceful	Pursue Dreams
I Care for Myself	I am Worthy	I am Powerful
I am Gifted	I am Fearless	Learning is Power
Explore More	Experience Life	Expand My Horizons
Passions I Cherish	My Ambitions	Future Plans
Goals to Reach	Find Joy	Build Friendships
Believe in Yourself	Choose Love	Explore Interests
I will Initiate	I will Discover	Keep Pushing
Enjoy Life	Seek Adventures	Stay True
Shine Bright	Education Matters	Embrace Each Day
Lead with Courage	Cultivate Creativity	Empower Each Other
Chase Excellence	Unlock Potential	Inspire Change

Thank You!

Have you ever given without expecting anything in return? If you have, you are aware of the tremendous rewards that can come from helping others. Not because it makes you a better person, but because it makes you feel good to know that you were able to improve someone else's life in some small way.

I want to give you this chance and ask you for a favor. In order for me to accomplish my mission of inspiring my readers to live their best lives, I first have to reach them. And the majority of people do evaluate a book based on its reviews. So, could you please take 3 minutes to post your honest review of this book on Amazon? With your help, this book will reach more people and assist them in achieving their goals and dreams. Just find this book on Amazon and write a few short words (or long words, I won't judge).

P.S. If you believe this book will benefit someone you know, please let them know about it too.

To your success,

Kalishia Winston

Made in United States
Orlando, FL
15 June 2025